FINGER WEAVING: INDIAN BRAIDING

BY ALTA R. TURNER

CHEROKEE PUBLICATIONS
CHEROKEE, NORTH CAROLINA

FOR YOUR FREE CATALOG OF OVER 400
NATIVE AMERICAN
BOOKS, VIDEOS, AUDIO CASSETTES, MAPS, CRAFT KITS, ETC.
contact
CHEROKEE PUBLICATIONS
P.O. BOX 430
CHEROKEE NC 28719
Phone (828) 488-8856
FAX (828) 488-6934
Email cpubl@aol.com
See our WEB page at:
www.CherokeePub.com

Dedicated with deep appreciation to the memory of those early American Indian artist-craftsmen who, with extraordinary skill, imagination and integrity, first worked out the techniquees described in this book.

Diagrams by Alta Ann Parkins.

Photographs by Leonard C. Turner, except for the Peruvian Paracas band on page 20, taken by Junius Bird, and the Basket Maker sashes on page 5, taken by Gilbert Wenger.

Copyright © 1973 by Sterling Publishing Co., Inc., New York, N.Y.

Reprinted in 1989 by
CHEROKEE PUBLICATIONS
P.O. BOX 430
CHEROKEE, NC 28719

Manufactured in the United States of America   All rights reserved
Library of Congress Catalog Card No.: 72-95200
Cherokee Publications ISBN 0-935741-13-5
(Previously ISBN 0-8069-5264-4)

Contents

Before You Begin 4
   Methods and Materials

Diagonal Stripe Pattern for Belt 7
   Preparation . . . Start Weaving . . . Making Fringe . . .
   To Make a Collar

Chevron Design 18
   Double Chevron . . . Additional Chevron Designs . . .
   Chevron Design for Neck-Tie . . . Another Neck-Tie
   Design

Diamond Design 28

Lightning Design 30

Double Lightning Design 32

Arrow-Head Design 34
   Preparation . . . Weaving

Peruvian Rep Braid (Multiple Wefts, Single Warps) . . . 36

Peruvian Cross Rep Braid (Multiple Wefts, Single Warps) . . 38

Peruvian Cross Rep with Three Colors 40

Peruvian Rep Braid (Multiple Wefts, Single Warps; Single
   Wefts, Multiple Warps) 42

Peruvian Cross Rep Braid (Multiple Wefts, Single Warps;
   Single Wefts, Multiple Warps) 45

After You Finish 46
   Bibliography

Index 48

The author gratefully acknowledges the help of Junius Bird, The American Museum of Natural History; Frederick F. Dockstader, Museum of the American Indian; Gilbert Wenger, Mesa Verde National Park Museum; Delia F. Castor, Ponca City Cultural Center and Indian Museum; Elsie Dillon and Patricia Barnes, The Montclair Art Museum; Mary Shell, Cherokee weaver; Louise Romine; Alan Anderson; Emily Frantz; Olga Sarre; Ingrid Nygards-Kers; Birgit Hackl; Louisa Hellegers, Crafts Editor. Special thanks to Alta Ann Parkins and Leonard C. Turner.

The following illustrations have been reproduced with the permission of the following museums and individuals: Illus. 1, Illus. 2, Illus. 5—Museum of the American Indian; Illus. 3—Mesa Verde National Park, Colorado; Illus. 6, Illus. 7—Alta Ann Parkins; Illus. 13—Emily R. Franz; title page, Illus. 15—Mary Shell; front cover, Illus. 22—Alan Anderson; Illus. 26—Denver Art Museum; Illus. 28—American Museum of Natural History.

Before You Begin

Finger weaving, also defined as flat braiding, is a very old method of thread interlacement, surely predating the use of looms in most parts of the world. It is referred to as finger weaving because you use your fingers to pick up the vertical warp threads through which you pass the horizontal weft. Flat braiding bears little relationship to the familiar three-strand braid ordinarily associated with the term "braiding." In very early times, probably often for ceremonial use, braiding progressed from a utility craft to one showing great skill and aesthetic judgment. The early craftsmen advanced far beyond the type of braiding in which one thread crosses the others from upper left to lower right and another strand crosses from upper right to lower left.

There are not, however, many references available with directions for decorative braiding, so it has been necessary to study certain braiding techniques from the actual bands and sashes which can be seen in museum collections. Some of these bands, dating from A.D. 300, are in excellent condition and show the use of very fine-spun threads in beautiful color arrangements and designs.

Just as the structures of these decorative pieces are defined by different terms, such as finger weave or flat braid, over the centuries a number of different methods have been developed for achieving the designs. There are different ways for securing the warps, different ways for drawing the tension and different ways to do the actual weaving. In fact, although the term "finger weaving" has been applied to work practiced for centuries by primitive tribes using two sets of elements —namely separate vertical warps and separate horizontal wefts—this book concerns a type of finger weaving for which you use only one set of threads or yarns. The warp and weft are not separate elements as they always are in loom weaving.

People in many parts of the world have

Illus. 1. This Seneca Indian Assumption Sash is actually the double lightning design woven with multiple color changes.

Illus. 2 (left). This multiple diamond design was woven by a Creek Indian in Georgia in the 19th century. Notice the outline of white beads.

Illus. 3 (right). Sashes of the pre-historic Basket Maker period from the southwestern United States.

in the design. By such a method, a weaver was able to make many designs of a kind which appear not to have been made elsewhere. See Illus. 26 and 28 for examples of these exquisite Peruvian braids.

During the 18th and 19th centuries, North American Indians, especially the Woodland and Plains Indian tribes, developed a number of complex finger-weaving or braiding techniques using wool yarns. Even with only one set of threads, the Indians devised a two-color interlocking worked out techniques for weaving one set of threads with the fingers. In Peru, for example, as early as A.D. 300, intricate braided designs were being made. Some of the Peruvian methods of braiding, and therefore the designs also, were very different from methods and designs developed in North America. The Peruvian weaver worked out a system for using multiple wefts and sometimes multiple warps, with which he could cover or leave uncovered any color, as it was called for technique much like a method used in making tapestries; with this technique, it became possible to weave many new geometric designs for use in ceremonial sashes, garters and headbands.

The Indians of the north appear to have used, as a rule, one weft at a time, weaving it over and under a series of warp threads.

In certain valleys in Lapland, bands braided in a chevron design are wound round the tops of shoes to keep out the snow.

Arabs weave the chevron design with quite a different effect because of the general difference in color progressions and in the yarn itself. They make interesting fringes using small, differently colored tassles with contrasting fringe wrappings. In the Orient, decorative braiding has been practiced for many centuries, and fine, silk flat braids are currently being made in Japan.

Directions in this book—limited to several designs made by North American Indians and to some of the designs made by ancient Peruvians—show you one way to do finger weaving or flat braiding. By following the step-by-step directions, you will learn to weave belts, hair ties, collars, neck-ties and dress or skirt trimming bands. Most instructions are for long narrow bands, but as you progress, the technical knowledge and experience you gain should lead you to create new designs or combinations of designs. As you discover numerous ways to arrange your colors, keep in mind that light and dark contrasts accentuate the pattern and that closely related colors result in a more subdued, blended design.

Methods and Materials

To finger weave, you begin with a definite number of warp threads which you also use, in a definite order, as the weft threads. When you pick up a warp thread to use it as a weft, you should always be aware of its function as a weft. Then, just as you used the warp as a weft, you drop the weft back, in a definite order, into the warp to use it again as a warp. If you unwove the weaving, the result would be, of course, only a single set of parallel vertical threads.

The opening through which you pass the weft is called the shed. The name "finger weaving" also applies here because you use your fingers instead of a shuttle—as in loom weaving—to draw the weft through the shed.

Except for a $\frac{1}{4}$″-wide, 6″-long dowel and a safety-pin, there is no intervening, expensive equipment in finger weaving to come between you, the craftsman, and your medium. The absence of cumbersome tools makes finger weaving a mobile craft which you can pursue even while travelling. A few strands of colorful yarns and some degree of concentration are all you need to provide hours of pleasure and satisfaction.

Four-ply wool knitting yarn, readily available in yarn shops and department stores, is suitable for finger weaving the 16 designs explained in this book. As you become proficient in the craft, you will be able to experiment with yarns of various sizes and spins, as well as with original designs and projects.

Diagonal Stripe Pattern for Belt

Preparation

Select three contrasting colors of four-ply knitting yarn. Cut 10 2½-yard lengths of each selected color: A, B and C. Arrange each color in a solid stripe on a ¼" dowel 6" long in the following order: 10A 10B 10C, looping the middle of each length of yarn round the dowel (see Illus. 10). Dividing the length of yarn in the middle makes it possible for you to work with a shorter length when weaving and eliminates the thread entanglement which would occur if you started the weaving at one end instead of in the middle.

Tie a piece of yarn round the 30 threads at a point just above the dowel and, with a safety-pin placed at this tie, secure the warp to a small pillow (see Illus. 10). The lengths above the dowel will be the second half of the belt.

Start Weaving

Step 1: In front of the dowel, start with the left outside thread placing it under the second thread and then over and under succeeding threads to the right. Place this first weft up under the dowel on the right as you must weave it with the second weft to start the right selvage (selvedge).

NOTE: It is very important to keep the order of the threads in parallel lines. Do not allow the warp threads to cross out of position.

Alternate strands always go up for each shed or division; the strands which are up in the first shed are down in the second shed. Make a shed by picking up the odd warp threads on your left forefinger, and draw the weft through this shed to the right. Then pull the separated threads in opposite directions to pack the preceding wefts into place.

Step 2: When the second thread is woven to the right, pull the first thread, which you previously put under the dowel, down around the second thread and into the warp to form the selvage. The first weft thread now becomes the right thread of the warp. As the weft threads return to the warp on the right, pull them free from the remaining warp threads to avoid large entanglements. Continue to weave from left to right.

As the work progresses, advance the safety-pin in the weaving to maintain good tension. Examine the belt critically and adjust any looseness in the work. To make a firm belt, you must place the wefts rather close to each other. They should be *well covered* by the warp threads.

Keep the left selvage a bit loose and weave each weft securely into the right selvage, pulling it into a straight line. Otherwise, the weaving will curve.

When the weft thread no longer reaches to the right of the dowel, you may hook it round the end of the safety-pin.

Illus. 4. For an unusual gift, make a diagonal design belt and matching collar. Strikingly colored yarns emphasize the diagonal pattern.

Illus. 5 (right). With some practice, perhaps you will be able to weave a double diamond design as seen in this Osage Indian sash. The border outline is white beads.

Illus. 6. Part of the beauty of finger-woven belts is in the choice of colors. This dramatic belt is woven in the diagonal design and its reverse. Simply reverse the direction of the diagonal at the end of the pattern.

Illus. 7 (right). After you master the basic diamond design technique, an interesting variation you can weave is a belt such as this one which is not rigidly repetitive in design.

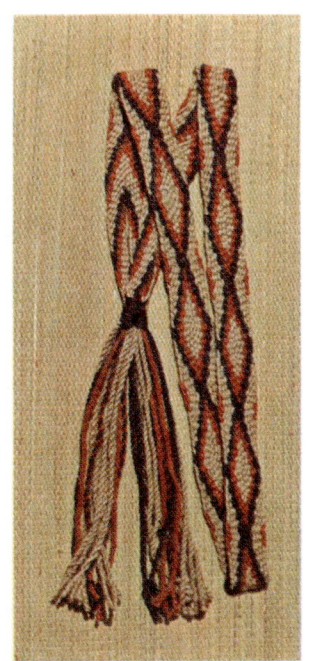

Illus. 8. You can make a more complicated belt by arranging and working two diamonds on your dowel, as was done here.

Illus. 9. This is the diamond pattern which will result if you weave following the directions on page 28.

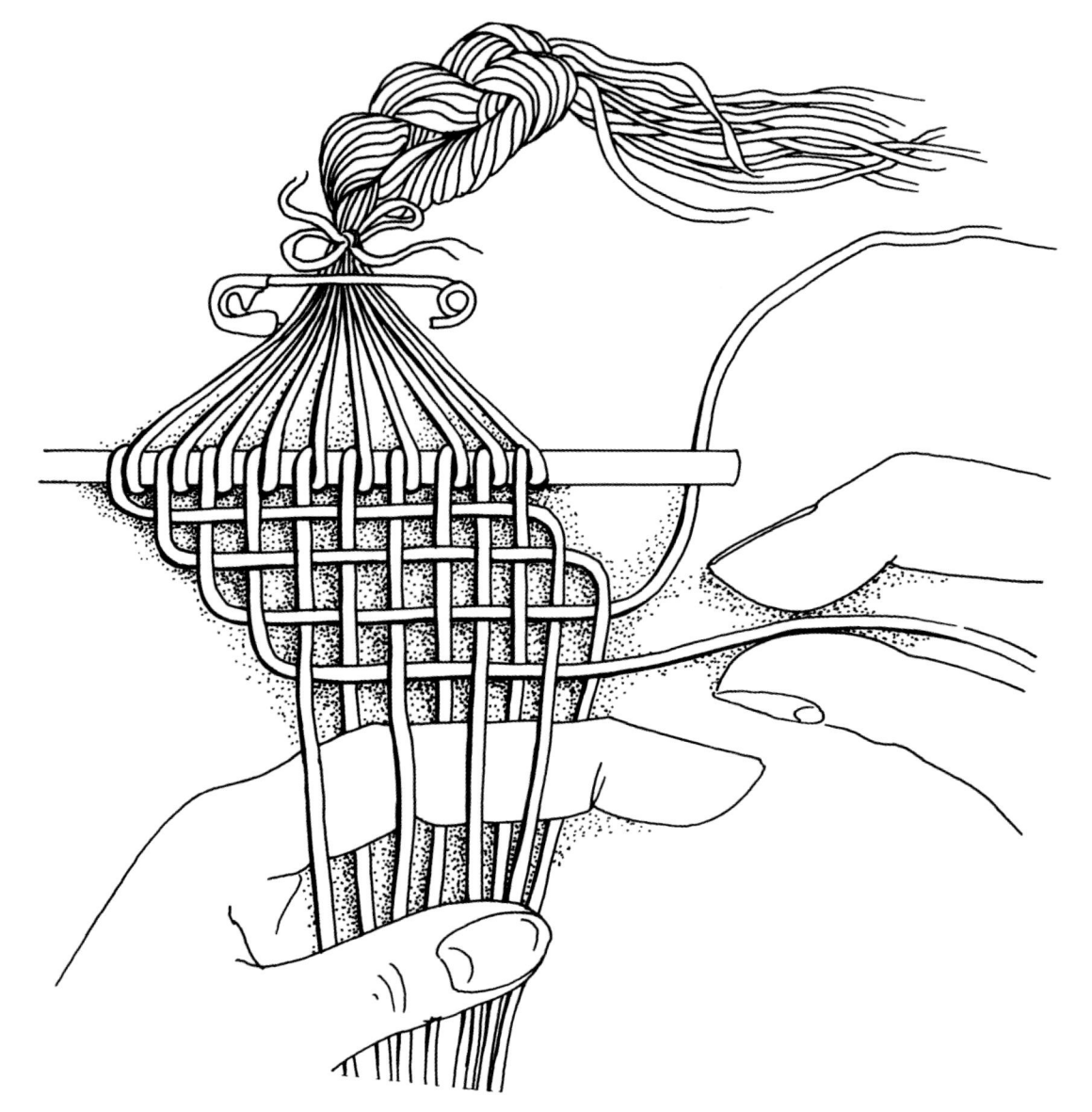

Step 3: Continue weaving in the same way, always weaving from left to right, with each succeeding outside left thread going under the adjacent thread and then over and under the remaining threads to the right, continuing to the desired length (see Illus. 11).

Step 4: In order to continue the diagonal stripes in the same direction when weaving the second half of the belt, re-pin the belt to the pillow at a point near the dowel and then remove the dowel. Take a firm hold of the loose half of the threads and pull the loops straight. Turn the belt around. Be sure you are turning the work *around*, not over.

Step 5: Weave with the left outside thread to the right selvage. Repeat with each following left thread, straightening the selvages at intervals to avoid curves in the belt. Continue until the second half is the same length as the first half.

Illus. 11. For the diagonal design, take each left thread under the adjacent right thread and then over and under a shed to the right edge.

Illus. 10. Diagram for the diagonal design. Loop the middle of each length of yarn round the dowel, tie a piece of yarn round the threads, and pin to a small pillow.

Illus. 12. This attractive belt is a chevron pattern taken from an old Lapp band.

Illus. 13. Not all belts need to have a fringe. This chevron belt was handsomely completed with a buckle instead.

Illus. 14. Weaving the chevron design is like weaving the diagonal design from the center in both directions—first to the right and then to the left.

Illus. 15. This lively belt with a double chevron pattern was woven by a Cherokee Indian who demonstrates finger weaving in Cherokee, North Carolina.

Illus. 16. Are you a father, son or brother who does not wear vividly colored belts? Make yourself a chevron design tie!

Illus. 17. If this double chevron design strikes your fancy, see page 23 for instructions.

Making Fringe

The Indians often braid these belts to the exact waist measurement and then make a long fringe for tying.

Step 6: You can make fringes in different ways: you can braid three or four strands or ply two or four ends.

To ply two ends, take the first one between your thumb and forefinger and twist tightly (until it kinks) to the right. Place a clip clothes pin on the end of the twisted strand and then place it where it will not unwind—under the edge of the pillow will do. Now, twist the second thread tightly to the right. Then pull both ends firmly together, at the same time removing the clothes pin. Start the two ends twisting to the left. The two easily ply. You may ply each pair of ends in the same way. Tie a knot at the end of each plied pair of threads and cut the fringe to an even line at the bottom. The diagonal pattern belts in Illus. 4 and 6 have plied ends.

Press the belt with a damp cloth with the iron gauge set at "wool." Your first woven creation is completed.

Illus. 18. A long fringe adds extra character to your creation. This belt is the diagonal pattern and its reverse.

To Make a Collar

Cut 30 threads, 10 each in the same three colors you used for the belt, each 1½ yards long. Arrange the threads on the dowel—10A 10B 10C.

Step 1: Start the weaving by proceeding in the same manner as for the belt (see page 7) *except that* you should pull the left selvage tightly into a curve and keep the right selvage loose.

Step 2: To weave the second half of the collar, turn the work *over* (not *around* as for the belt) and start from the left again. The diagonal lines then converge at the center, making the curve of the collar run in one circular direction (see Illus. 19).

Step 3: Ply each pair of warp ends for a short fringe. Tie the collar in front or back.

Once you have become an expert in weaving the diagonal design, you can experiment. Try, for instance, reversing the direction of the diagonal at the end of the pattern (see Illus. 6).

Illus. 19. Make a diagonal pattern collar as you did the belt except that you must pull the left selvage securely to form a curve. Keep the right selvage loose.

Illus. 20 (left). Vibrant colors and the striking lightning design combine to create this outstanding belt.

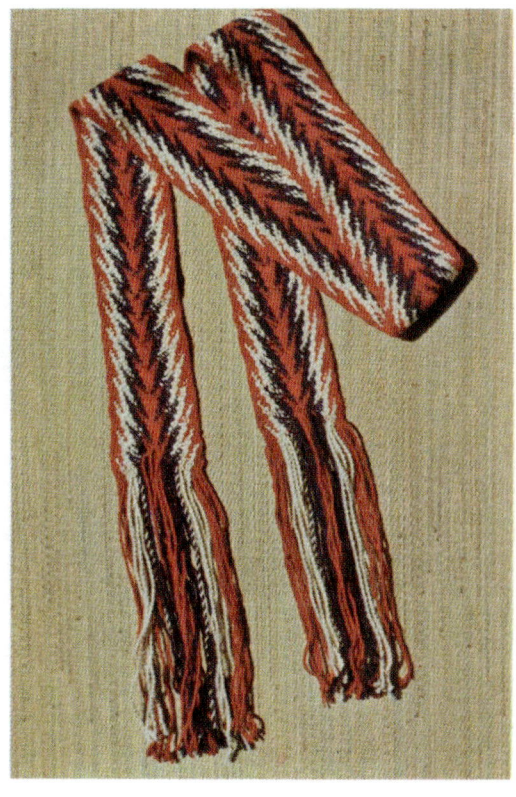

Illus. 21 (right). You can weave a double lightning design quite simply after you learn the lightning. The process is exactly the same, except that you weave in both directions—first to the right and then to the left—for the double lightning. This example, however, also includes several additional interlocking changes.

Illus. 22. This wide sash, also pictured on the front cover, was woven in a triple arrow-head design by a student who learned the finger-weaving technique from a Sauk-Fox Indian.

Illus. 23. Arrow-heads seem to be a natural design for Indian braided items. Directions for this pattern are on pages 34–35.

Chevron Design

For this design, you need 2½-yard lengths of yarn in four colors.

Step 1: Cut four lengths of the lightest color D, six lengths of the next lightest color C, four lengths of a darker color B, and six lengths of the darkest color A.

Arrange the lengths on the dowel as you did on page 7, with the lightest color in the middle and the other three colors in a progression of light to dark with the darkest color on the outside, as follows: 3A 2B 3C 4D 3C 2B 3A.

Step 2: Tie a piece of yarn round the 20 threads above the dowel and secure with a safety-pin to a pillow.

Step 3: Locate the middle of the group of threads in front of the dowel—it is in the middle of the center color. The first thread you weave is the D thread left of center. With your left

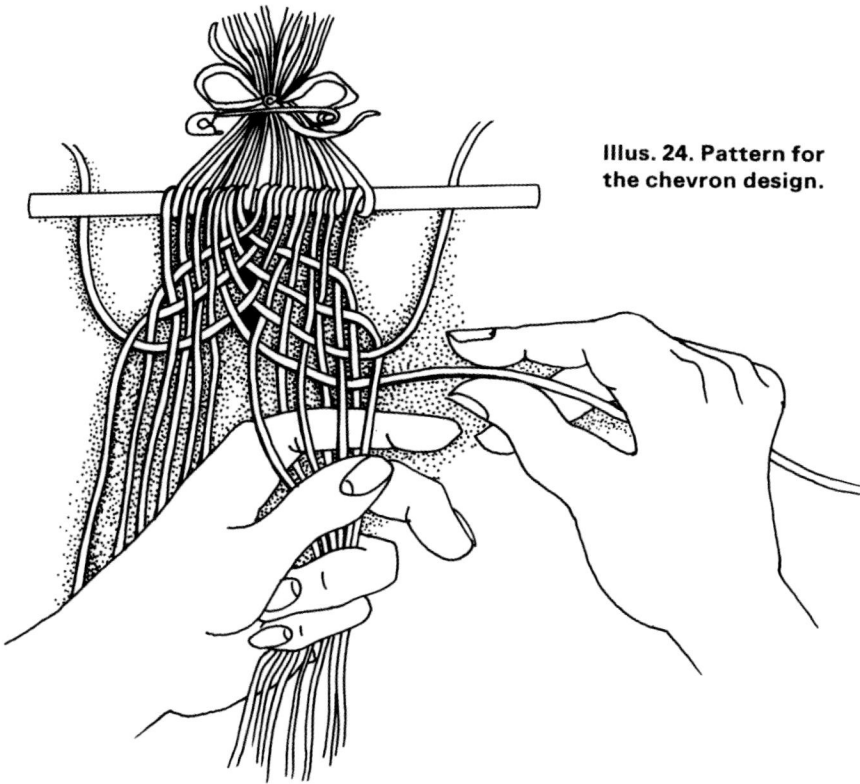

Illus. 24. Pattern for the chevron design.

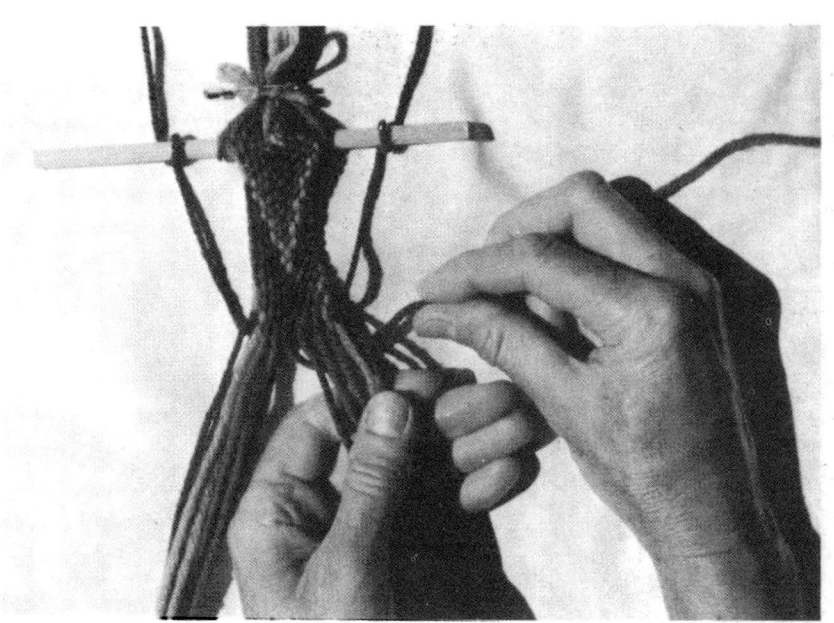

Illus. 25. Here, the up left-of-center thread moves to the right through the shed. The selvage threads are shown on each side of the dowel.

forefinger, starting in the center and moving towards the right, pick up a shed of the odd numbered threads 1, 3, 5, and so on. With your right hand, pull the D thread left of the center through the shed to the right and place it under the dowel (see Illus. 24). Later, you use this thread to start the selvage with the second weft thread.

Step 4: Pick up a shed from the center towards the left edge, odd threads up, and draw the D thread right of center through the shed to the left. Place this first weft on the left side up under the dowel so that you can use it with the second weft to start the left selvage.

NOTE: The left of center thread always crosses to the right and the right of center thread always crosses to the left.

Be sure to keep the warp threads in the proper order.

Step 5: Now, weave the next thread left of center, an up thread, under the adjacent right thread and through the shed, with the odd numbered warps up, to the right edge. Pull the first weft, which is under the dowel, down round the second weft to start the selvage, and place the second weft up under the dowel.

Step 6: Pack each weft into place by pulling the upper and lower separated warps of the shed in opposite directions.

Weave the thread right of center, an up thread, under the adjacent left thread and through the shed, with the odd numbered warps up, towards the left edge. Pull the first weft which is under the dowel down round the second weft to start

Illus. 26 (left). This is an ancient Peruvian braid from the Paracas or Nazca civilizations.

Illus. 27 (right). This unusual braid, fashioned on the ancient Peruvian braid above, though only in three colors, exhibits the Peruvian rep technique.

Illus. 28. This ancient Peruvian (Paracas) band displays the cross rep technique.

Illus. 29. This Peruvian cross rep band was copied from the prehistoric Paracas band in Illus. 28.

Illus. 30. For a more subdued belt, use subtler colors, such as the grey, black and white which were used for this chevron pattern.

the selvage and place the second weft up under the dowel.

Step 7: Pull each weft firmly in a horizontal direction to the right or to the left. This helps cover the wefts by the threads in the warp position. You should hardly have to pull the threads in the vertical position except to straighten selvages and to remove a possible loop.

Step 8: Continue weaving first with the up left-of-center thread moving to the right and then with the up right-of-center thread moving to the left (see Illus. 25).

Advance the safety-pin as you weave in order to have proper tension on the warps as you work.

When the work progresses to the point where it is difficult to reach the dowel with the selvage threads, you may be able to place them under the end of the safety-pin. If not, add two extra safety-pins—one on each side of the safety-pin that secures the work to the pillow—and catch the selvage threads round these pins. In this way, you can easily see where the selvage threads are at all times.

If or when you find you have made a mistake in your work, such as not weaving in a selvage thread, not keeping the alternating sheds in order, or picking up the wrong weft, you need to go back *at once* to make corrections. Finger weaving calls for precise work and you cannot proceed with a design until you have corrected any errors.

Step 9: Weave to the desired length and make fringe as on page 14.

Step 10: Adjust the safety-pin back to a near-center position and remove the tie round the remaining half of the warp. Remove the dowel, straighten the loops and weave from the left of center to the right edge, and then from the right of center to the left edge. The chevrons now reverse to form a diamond in the middle of the belt. Finish the belt and press.

As you can see, the general directions which you must use for all finger weaving patterns—that is, removing the dowel and pulling out the loops at the half-way point, making the fringe, pressing the weaving when finished—are fairly routine. As a result, from here on, these general directions will not always be repeated in each succeeding lesson.

Double Chevron

As you become more experienced, you could try to weave a double chevron pattern, as shown in Illus. 15 and 17.

Just as you would suppose, you arrange two chevrons on the dowel instead of one, and weave first to the right and then to the left with the left chevron. Then weave first to the right and then to the left with the right chevron. Repeat for your desired length. You will be pleased to discover how the threads cross over in the middle, weaving a unit instead of two separate chevrons.

Additional Chevron Designs

An interesting experiment is for you to try the following asymmetrical color progression for the chevron design using 40 warp threads as follows: 8A 2E 8B 4E 8C 2E 8D. When you consolidate the color areas on the dowel, each color alternates from one side of the center to the other side as you weave. As the work progresses, each color develops into an elongated rhomboid. Two rhomboids of two different colors—A and D and B and C—converge to form the chevron (see Illus. 31). The E color outlines and emphasizes the separate color areas.

To weave, find the center of the warp in the middle of the 4E group. Start to weave towards the right with the left-of-center E thread. Then weave towards the left with the right-of-center E thread. Continue as in the first chevron directions on pages 18–22.

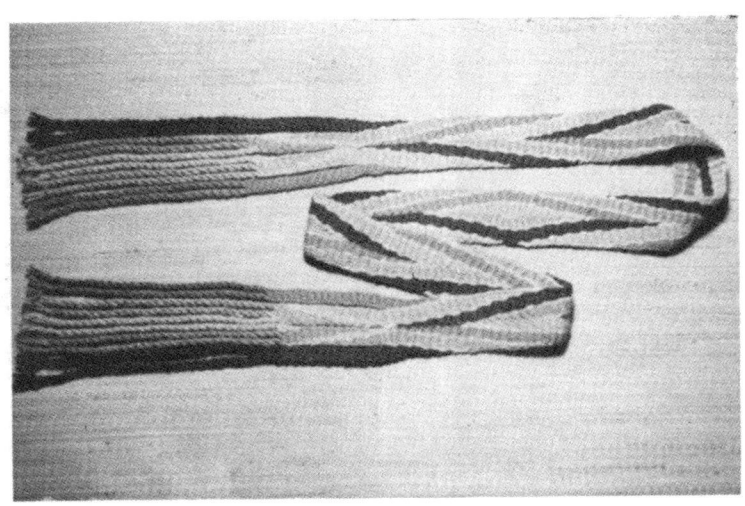

Illus. 31. Vary the chevron pattern by experimenting with the color arrangement of your yarn. This unusual design is one possibility.

Illus. 32. This splendid Peruvian rep braid was masterfully woven in vibrant colors.

Illus. 33. You can make many color patterns when you weave the Peruvian cross rep technique.

Illus. 34. Another interesting chevron variation based on color arrangement.

You could also try a color arrangement with four solid color areas, without using the outlining color, as follows: 5A 5B 5C 5D (see Illus. 34). If you wish to weave a wider belt, arrange the yarn as follows: 10A 10B 10C 10D.

To weave, first find the center of the warp threads which is between the B and C groups. Start to weave towards the right with the left-of-center B thread. Then weave towards the left with the right-of-center C thread.

Continue as for the first chevron.

A third chevron variation is a development of the band design which comes from a valley in Lapland. The Lapp design has a plain colored area and a light-dark alternating warp area symmetrically arranged on each side of the center.

The design shown in Illus. 35, however, has the alternating light and dark warps on one side of the center with an asymmetrical solid colored area on the other side of the center.

The color arrangement, with 26 warp threads—13 on each side of the center—is as follows: 13A 2B 1C 1B 1C 1B 1C 1B 1C 1B 1C 2B.

Find the center of the warp, between the 13A and the 2B threads. Begin to weave towards the right with the left-of-center A thread. Then weave to the left with the right-of-center B thread. Continue weaving in turn, from left to right, the 13A threads alternating with the 13B and C threads, from the right to the left.

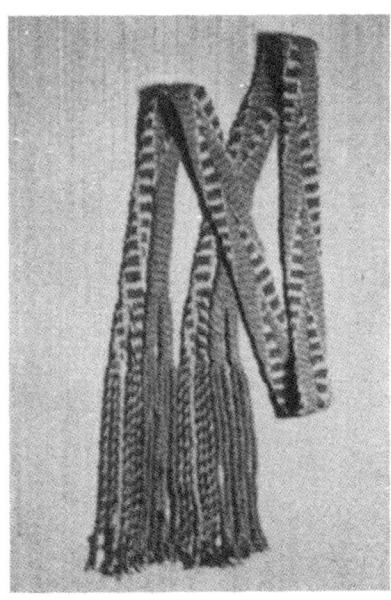

Illus. 35. This pattern is developed from a Lapp pattern. Try it, or be imaginative and design an original variation.

Chevron Design for Neck-Tie

After you learn to do the chevron design neatly and with an even tension, you are ready to weave a neck-tie like those in Illus. 16.

Step 1: Cut 24 threads $2\frac{1}{4}$ yards long, using two colors. On the dowel arrange 12 threads of color A followed by 12 threads of color B.

Step 2: Weaving the narrow end of the tie first, make about four patterns or chevrons exactly as you did on pages 18–22. Find the center of the warp threads and weave the A thread left of center through the shed made of color B to the right edge. Then, picking up the B thread right of center, weave to the left edge through a shed of color A.

The design, because of the color arrangement, is one of alternating rhomboid shapes, which you can see in color on page 13.

Step 3: After you have woven four patterns, or about eight inches from the center for the neckband, measure a length of yarn of each color twice as long as the remaining unwoven threads.

Step 4: Place the middle of the matching length of yarn over and under the two right outside warp threads—the selvage threads (see Illus. 36).

Step 5: Add the matching double length of warp on the left side, looping it over and under the two selvage threads. In this way, you increase the width of the neck-tie by two warp threads at a time on each side.

Step 6: Keeping these added warps pushed up to the other warps as closely and neatly as possible, continue to weave another chevron pattern.

Step 7: Increase again, in the same way, at the end of this pattern by adding a double warp at each selvage.

Illus. 36. To increase for the neck-tie shape, add a length of yarn to the outside warp threads.

Continue increasing at the end of each pattern until you reach the desired length—which is about 24 inches from the middle. You should have increased the number of warps from 12 to 18 or 20 on each side of the lower end of the tie.

Step 8: Now, turn the work around and weave one pattern only towards the front with the original 24 warps.

Step 9: In order to make the front of the tie wider than the back, weave only one chevron pattern before starting to increase the width with two warps on each side. Then, increase in the same way at the end of each pattern and also at the middle of each pattern. You need to increase seven or eight times to end up with 26 or 28 warp ends of each color.

Step 10: Ply each two ends of warp for a short fringe at each end and trim to a V. Then, knot each ply and press.

Another Neck-Tie Design

You may wish to try outlining two colors—A and B—for a neck-tie like the one in Illus. 37. To do this, arrange the warp on a dowel as follows: 7A 6B 7C.

Find the middle of the warp threads in the center of the 6B threads. Start to weave towards the right with the B thread that is left of center. Then weave towards the left with the right-of-center B thread. Continue to weave as you did for the first neck-tie. To shape this tie as you weave, however, increase the warps only with colors A and C.

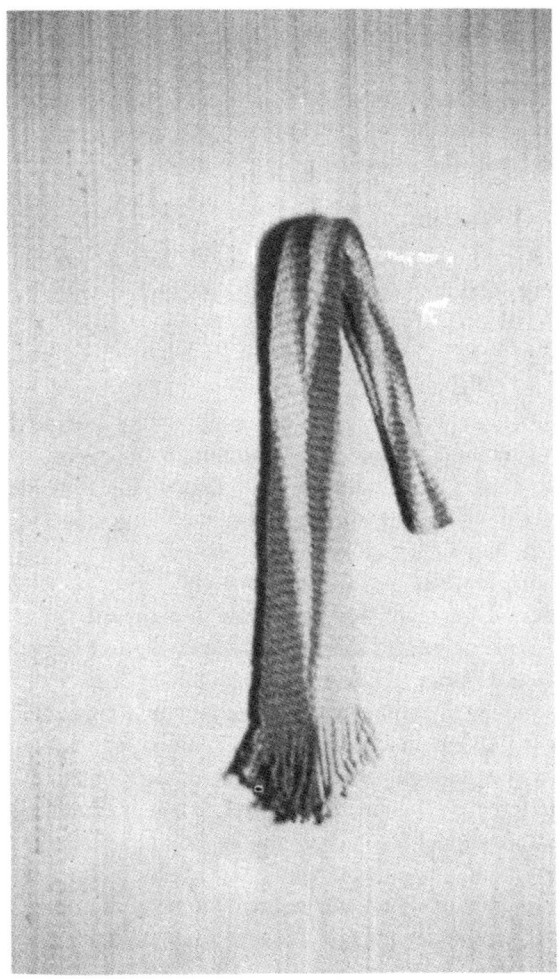

Illus. 37. Altering the yarn order in the neck-tie also produces an interesting chevron variation for you to weave.

Diamond Design

You make the diamond design by weaving the chevron and then reversing the process by weaving from the outside to the middle.

Preparation

Arrange on your dowel 24 threads $2\frac{1}{2}$ yards long in three colors, using the following order: 3A 3B 12C 3B 3A. Secure to pillow.

Weaving

Step 1: Find the center of the warp threads and pick up a shed of the threads to the right of the center, odd threads up. Draw the thread left of the center through the shed towards the right edge. Place it under the dowel.

Step 2: Pick up a shed from the center to the left, odd threads up, and draw the thread right of center through the shed towards the left edge. Place it under the dowel.

Step 3: Continue with this chevron technique, as on pages 18–22, until the 3A warps originally on the right and the 3A warps originally on the left have reached the center. Then weave the first A thread located to the right of the center over, under and over the 3A threads to the left of the center. Then weave the next right A under, over and under the left 3A, and finally weave the last right A as you did the first. The 3A right-of-center warps should cross to the left. Without this crossing of the center threads, there would be a slit in the center of the work where you begin to reverse the chevron for the diamond (see Illus. 38).

Step 4: Now start to weave, using the same general procedure, but with the outside right B warp, weaving towards the center. Then weave with the outside left B warp, weaving towards the center. Continue to weave, alternating from the right and left sides towards the center, always crossing the two center threads in the same over and under pattern.

When the 12C warps are in the center again, as they were at the beginning, begin to weave from the center to the outside as for the chevron on pages 18–22.

Step 5: Alternate weaving the chevron design and the reverse to the desired length. Then turn the work around, remove the dowel and weave the second half of the belt in the same way.

NOTE: It may be more difficult to gain an even tension when weaving the reverse of the chevron —that is, when you are weaving from the outside towards the center. As with all of the other techniques, you must, therefore, examine your work frequently for necessary straightening of selvages and to tighten loose threads.

Illus. 38. This close-up of the basic diamond braid shown in color in Illus. 9 shows the crossing of the six center threads before reversing the pattern. Other fine examples of the diamond design are the Creek Indian sash in Illus. 2 and the Osage sash in Illus. 5.

Lightning Design

This design makes use of an interlocking technique. The work progresses from left to right with three colors—A, B, C—as for the diagonal design on page 7. In each row of weaving from left to right, one A thread interlocks with one B thread and this B thread interlocks with a C thread.

Step 1: Arrange on a dowel eight ends, each 2½ yards long, of three colors in the following order: 8A 8B 8C. Place the lightest or brightest color between the two darker colors or place the darkest or brightest color between the two lighter colors.

Step 2: You create this pattern by moving the wefts from left to right. Begin with the left thread of color A. Carry it under the second left thread and then over and under succeeding threads as far as the fourth thread of color B, counting from the left. Interlock the A weft with this fourth B thread as shown in Illus. 39, returning the A color to the warp in place of the fourth B.

Step 3: Continue to weave under and over with the B thread as far as the fourth thread of color C, counting from the left. In the same way as before, interlock the B weft with the fourth thread of color C. Return the B thread to the warp to take the place of the fourth C warp thread.

Step 4: Weave with the C thread to the right selvage and you have completed one row of the pattern. After you see what is required to interlock the threads, you should learn to pick up the shed on your forefinger, interlocking the two colors as you draw the weft through the shed.

Step 5: Now, with the left A thread, weave as far as the third B thread (counting from the left), interlock and continue with the third B thread as far as the third C. Interlock these two colors—the third B and the third C—and continue with the third C thread to the right selvage.

As you weave this second row of the pattern, you must be careful to weave the first interlocked A and B warps in the proper position. That first A warp, which was interlocked in the fourth B warp position, tends to fall out of line, as does the

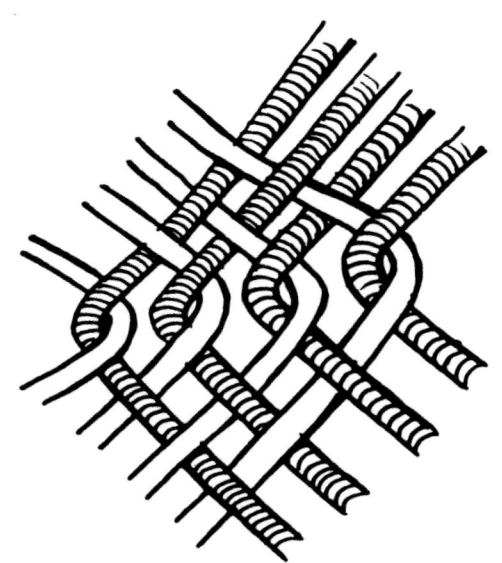

Illus. 39. Diagram of interlocking which you use in the lightning, double lightning and arrowhead techniques.

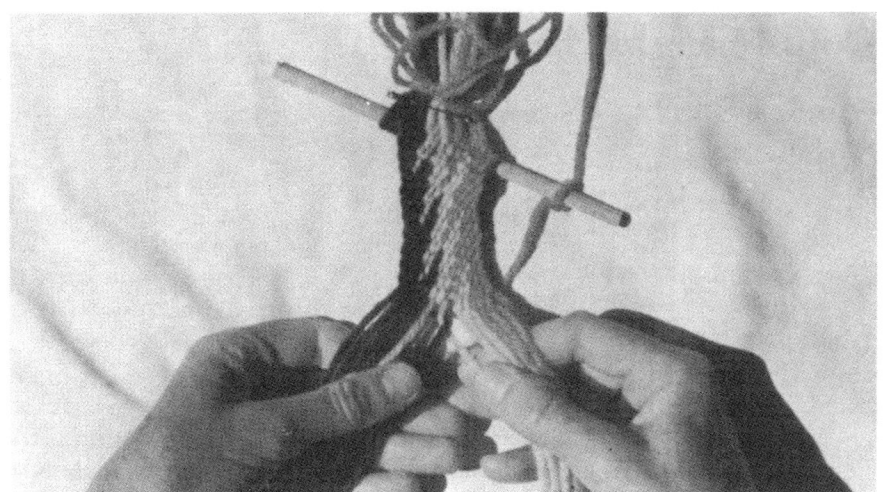

Illus. 40. This close-up shows the interlocking of the left A with the fourth B thread from the left.

interlocked B thread from its place where you interlocked the fourth C. Be sure to pull them into place.

Step 6: With the left A warp thread, weave as far as the second B thread, interlock and continue with the second B thread, weaving in the third and fourth A already there and on as far as the second C. Interlock the second B with the second C and continue with the second C to the right selvage.

Step 7: With the left A warp, weave as far as the first B thread, interlock and continue with the first B to the first C, weaving to the right selvage with the first C. Illus. 39 shows color A interlocked completely with color B.

Step 8: All of the colors are now in solid stripes again as they were at the beginning. Stop here to examine your work and to adjust any looseness in the weave. The warps should cover the wefts. The tension is difficult at first, but becomes more firm as you proceed. You have to adjust the interlocked threads especially to tighten the tension.

Step 9: Now repeat the interlocking of the left A with the fourth B and the fourth B with the fourth C. Next interlock the left A with the third B and the third B with the third C. As before, proceed by interlocking the left A with the second B and the second B with the second C. Then, to complete the pattern, interlock the left A with the first B and the first B with the first C. Examine and adjust the warp threads to cover the wefts.

Step 10: Weave to the desired length, leaving enough yarn at the end for a fringe.

Step 11: To make the second half, remove the dowel, turn the work around (*not over*). As you weave, the points of the design should all run in one direction.

Completed lightning design belts are shown in color on page 16.

Double Lightning Design

Careful practice of the lightning pattern on page 30 is necessary before you start to learn this technique.

Step 1: To make a double lightning belt like the one in Illus. 41, arrange yarn on a dowel as follows: 8A 8B 10C 8B 8A. Use 42 threads, each 2½ yards long.

Step 2: As for the chevron design on page 18, find the center of the warp threads, which is in the middle of the 10C threads. Start to weave with the C thread left of the center, moving *under* the adjacent right thread and then over and under succeeding threads to the fourth thread of color B, counting from the left. Interlock (see page 30), drop C into the warp and continue with the fourth B thread as far as the fourth A thread, counting from the left. Drop the B into the warp here and continue with the fourth A to the selvage, placing the A up under the dowel (see Illus. 41).

Step 3: Now carry the C thread right of center *under* the adjacent left thread and then over and under succeeding threads as far as the fourth B thread, counting from the right. Interlock, drop the C into the warp here and continue to the left with the B thread as far as the fourth A, counting from the right. Interlock the fourth B with the fourth A and continue to the left selvage, placing the A thread under the dowel.

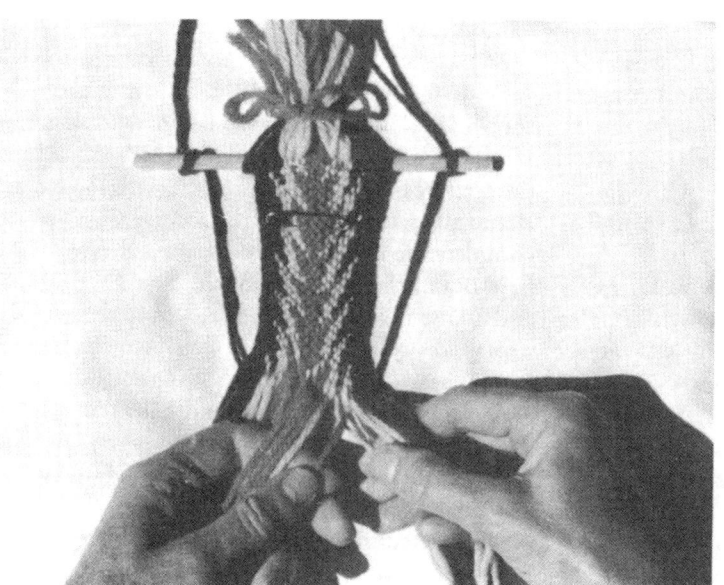

Illus. 41. Close-up of the interlocking of the left-of-center C thread with the fourth B thread counting from the left.

You have now made one row of the pattern from the center to the right and from the center to the left.

Step 4: Pick up a shed, odd threads up—1, 3, 5, and so on—to the right of the center, taking care to draw the C-interlocked thread, and, farther along, the B-interlocked thread, into the proper position in the shed. Draw the up C thread left of center through the shed to the right as far as the third B thread. Interlock and carry the third B thread to the third A. Interlock and draw the third A thread to the right, making the selvage as you have learned (see page 7) with the A thread already there.

Step 5: Now pick up a shed towards the left, odd threads up, taking care to draw the C and B interlocked threads into the proper position in the shed. Draw the up C thread right of center through the shed to the left as far as the third B. Interlock the C with the third B and carry the third B to the third A. Interlock the third B with the third A, continuing with the third A to the left edge. Start the selvage with the A thread under the dowel. This ends the second row of this pattern.

Step 6: Carefully pick up a shed of every other thread from the center to the right and draw the C thread left of center, an up thread, through the shed as far as the second thread of color B. Interlock and continue with the B thread to the second thread of color A. Interlock the second B with the second A and continue to the right selvage with the second A.

Step 7: Now do the same from the center to the left, weaving with the first C thread, an up thread, right of center. Interlock with the second B carrying the second B along to interlock with the second A.

Continue with the second A to left selvage.

Step 8: Moving to the right again, pick up a shed and draw the C thread left of center, an up thread, through the shed to the right, interlocking with the first B thread. Continue with the B thread to interlock with the first A and on with the A to the selvage.

Step 9: Make a shed on the left side and draw the C thread, an up thread, right of center through as far as the first B thread. Interlock and carry the B thread to the left to interlock with the first A thread. Weave with the A to the selvage. You have completed four rows. The center C threads cross in the center as they do in the chevron design (see page 19).

Step 10: Repeat these interlocking steps using threads 4, 3, 2, 1 of color B and color A, alternating first to the right and then to the left to the length desired.

Step 11: Remove the dowel, turn the work around, and weave the second half of the belt. The design of the second half moves in the opposite direction from the center in the same manner as the chevron does.

The double lightning design is sometimes woven to a width of 8 to 10 inches, with multiple color changes forming numerous converging forked lines on each side of the center. Such sashes (see Illus. 11), however, are difficult to make without considerable practice.

Other variations of design are possible if you use and interlock more threads of each color. This method results in thin and thick strokes to the lightning design.

Arrow-Head Design

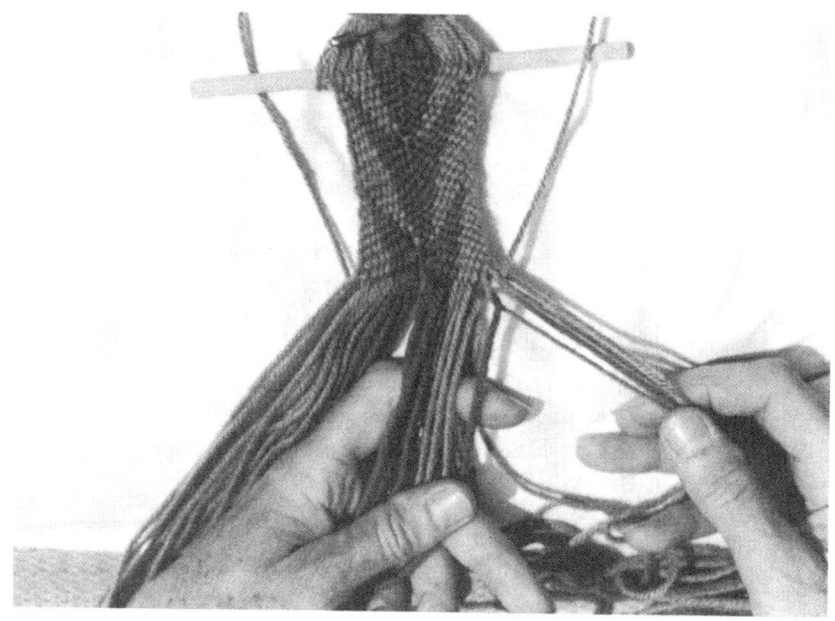

Illus. 42. Here, the interlocking of the B color with the ninth A has been completed on each side. The second interlocking of the B with the eighth A is just taking place, on the right first.

The arrow-head design utilizes the interlocking technique you learned for the lightning and double lightning designs (see page 30). Start weaving the belt from the middle, weaving first to the right and then to the left.

Preparation

Take two colors, A and B, $2\frac{1}{2}$ yards long, 18 threads of one color and 22 threads of the other. Distribute these threads on the dowel in the progression: 11A 18B 11A. Secure the work to a pillow with a safety-pin as before (see page 7).

Weaving

Find the center of the warp in the middle of the B threads.

Step 1: Pick up a shed from the center towards the right edge, odd numbered threads at the top of the shed (up). Draw the B thread which is left of center under the adjacent right thread through the shed moving to the right as far as the ninth A thread, counting from the left of the A group. Interlock the B thread with the ninth A thread and weave with that A thread on through to the right.

Step 2: Pick up a shed from the center to the left, with the odd numbered threads at the top of the shed. Draw the B thread which is right of center under the adjacent left thread through the shed moving to the left as far as the ninth A thread, counting from the right of the group. Interlock the B with the A thread and then weave with the A through the remaining A threads to the left. Now you have finished one row of the pattern.

Step 3: To continue the diagonal line of the arrow-head, make a shed from the center to the right edge, odd numbered warps up. Draw the B thread which is left of center, an up thread, through the shed to the right as far as the eighth A warp, counting from the left (see Illus. 42). Interlock the B weft with the A warp and continue with the A to the right. Start the selvage (see page 7) with the first A thread under the dowel.

Step 4: Make a shed from the center to the left, with the odd numbered warps up. Draw the B thread right of center, an up thread, through the shed moving to the left as far as the eighth A warp, counting from the right. Interlock the B weft with the A warp and continue with the A to the left. Start the selvage with the first A thread under the dowel. You have now interlocked twice on each side.

Step 5: To continue the converging right and left diagonal lines of the arrow-head, pick up the shed as before from the center towards the right edge, being careful to pull the two interlocked B threads into position in the warp. Draw the B thread left of center, an up thread, through the shed to the right as far as the seventh A warp, counting from the left. Interlock the B weft with the seventh A warp and continue with the A thread to the right selvage.

Step 6: Pick up a shed from the center towards the left, being careful to pull the two interlocked B warps into position. Draw the B thread right of center, an up thread, to the left as far as the seventh A warp, counting from the right. Interlock the B weft with the A warp and continue with the A thread to the selvage.

Stop to examine your work and pull the warps to an even tension. You probably need to tighten the three interlocked warps on each side. The converging diagonal lines of the design should begin to be evident. You can see that to continue the converging lines, you need to continue interlocking to the right and to the left using the remaining sixth, fifth, fourth, third, second and first A threads.

Step 7: After you have interlocked nine times on each side, your warp is in the same order as in the beginning. Then repeat the interlocking of the ninth, eighth, seventh, sixth, fifth, fourth, third, second, and first A threads on each side to the desired length.

Step 8: Remove the dowel and weave the second half of the belt. The arrow-heads move in a reverse direction.

For striking examples of arrow-head weaving, see page 17. Then, see what new designs you can create using double or triple arrow-heads.

Peruvian Rep Braid
(Multiple Wefts, Single Warps)

In this pattern, for which you learn one Peruvian method of braiding, you will see that half of the warp threads are never used as wefts and are never covered by wefts. The result is a zig-zag design along the full length of the belt. Illus. 43 shows the ancient Peruvian technique in which this zig-zag is evident.

This design calls for an equal number of dark and light threads and the number must be divisible by four.

Step 1: Arrange on a dowel 24 threads 2⅓ yards long from left to right as follows: 4 dark B, 4 dark C, 4 dark B, 12 light A.

Using the left group of 4 dark B threads as one weft, weave from left to right through a shed of 8 dark single warps and the 12 light single ones. Place the weft group on the pillow parallel to the dowel on the right.

Step 2: With the 4 threads of color C at the left, weave to the right through a shed of 4 dark B threads and the 12 light A ones. Place the second weft group below and parallel to the first weft group.

Step 3: With the last left group of 4 dark color B, weave to the right through a shed of the light A warp and place this weft group below and parallel to the others on the right.

Step 4: The next step is to weave with the top B group that is on the right and next to the dowel. Pick up the shed on your left forefinger begin-

Illus. 43. A dramatic zig-zag design evolves when you weave a Peruvian rep braid.

Illus. 44. Draw the upper right dark weft group to the left through a shed of the remaining 8 dark and 12 light threads.

ning with the left light A thread, continuing through the 12 light A threads and on through 8 of the dark threads: 4 dark B, 4 dark C. Draw the top dark B group through this shed to the left (see Illus. 44). With the separated warps, pack the wefts into position.

Step 5: Next, pick up the shed beginning with the left light A thread, continuing to the right through the 12 light A threads and the 4 dark B threads. Draw the dark C group at the upper right through the shed towards the left.

Step 6: Pick up the shed beginning with the left light A thread through the 12 light A threads only. Draw the last group of dark B threads through the shed from right to left. Pack the wefts into place and adjust any loose threads.

Now all of the dark threads are on the left as they were in the beginning.

Step 7: Weave following directions in Steps 1, 2 and 3 as you did the first time through.

Continue weaving with the three dark groups from left to right. When the three dark groups are on the right again, weave from right to left as you did in Steps 4, 5 and 6.

Step 8: When you have finished the first half of the belt, remove the dowel and the string round the upper half of the warp. Pull out the loops and follow the same pattern for weaving the second half.

After you learn this technique you may wish to arrange a belt with wider light and dark bands. You could also arrange to have the dark warps zig-zag through the center of the design. See Illus. 26 and 27 for inspiration for possible Peruvian rep braids.

Peruvian Cross Rep Braid
(Multiple Wefts, Single Warps)

You observed in the preceding chapter that you can easily cover a group of wefts woven together as one by weaving them over and under single warps. This fact is useful in making original designs. In this design, you first cross groups of threads in the middle of the braid, instead of moving them directly from one selvage to the other.

For the simplest design to weave to learn this technique, try 8 dark threads and 8 light threads—each 1⅔ yards long.

Step 1: Arrange the threads in following order on the dowel: 4 dark threads, 8 light threads, 4 dark threads. Tie a piece of thread round the upper warp and secure it to a pillow with a safety-pin.

Step 2: Pick up the 4 left dark threads and weave under and over the left 4 light threads, placing the 4 dark threads on the left side of the center between the light threads.

Step 3: Pick up the 4 right dark threads and weave through the 4 right light threads and on

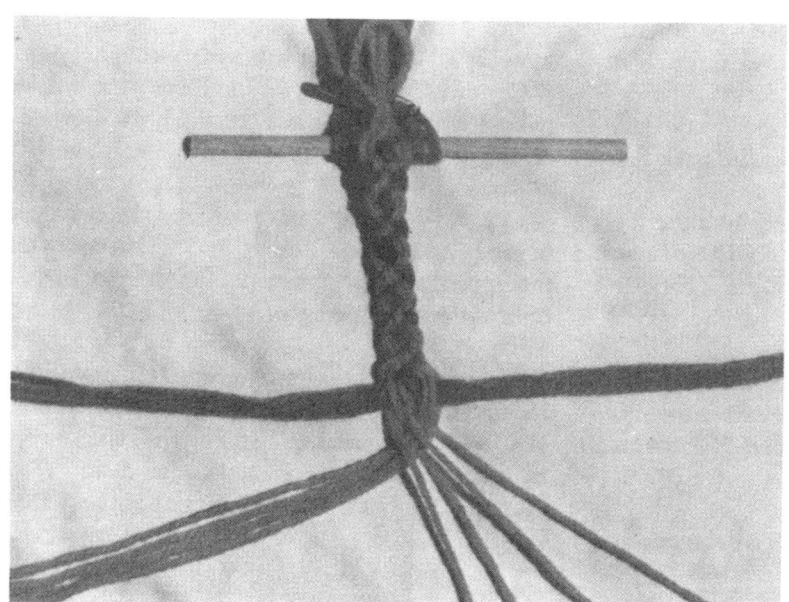

Illus. 45. In a two-color Peruvian cross rep braid with multiple wefts and single warps, each color crosses in the center.

through the 4 dark threads you already placed at left center. You have now made the first center cross of dark threads.

Step 4: To make the center cross of light threads, first make a shed of the 4 left light threads. You have 2 threads above and 2 threads below your left forefinger. Draw the left group of 4 dark threads through this shed to the left, leaving 4 light threads left of center.

Step 5: Do the same with the right group, making a shed with the 4 right light threads and drawing the 4 dark threads through the shed to the right.

Step 6: Now make a shed of the 4 light threads left of center and draw the 4 right light threads to the left through the shed to make a cross (see Illus. 45).

The light threads are the covering threads in this pattern and the dark groups show only at the selvage and where they cross each other in the center.

Step 7: Continue making the alternate light and dark center crosses in this manner, making the shed always with the light groups of 4 threads, except where the two dark groups cross each other in the center.

This procedure makes a narrow band suitable for trimming the neck-line of a dress or blouse.

Peruvian Cross Rep with Three Colors

(Multiple Wefts, Single Warps)

For the design in Illus. 46, use 16 threads of one color and 8 threads each of two other colors. The dominant color (the one with 16 threads) is the covering color in this design. Use each thread of the dominant color singly, except when the color crosses with itself in the center.

Step 1: Arrange on a dowel $2\frac{1}{2}$-yard lengths of colors A, B, C, as follows: 8A 4B 8C 4B 8A. Pick up a shed from the left to the center using 8A 4B 4C. Draw the right 4C threads through the shed to the left.

Step 2: Pick up a shed from the right using 8A 4B and draw the remaining 4C threads through the shed to the right. This crosses the C threads.

Step 3: Pick up a shed with the left 4C 8A and 4B and draw the right 4B threads through the shed to the upper left.

Step 4: Pick up a shed with the right 4C 8A threads and draw the remaining 4B threads through the shed to the upper right. This makes the cross of color B.

Step 5: Pick up a shed with the 8 left color A and draw the 4 near right color A group through the shed to the left.

Step 6: Pick up the reverse shed with the same 8 left color A threads and draw the 4 right remaining color A threads through this shed to the left. You have now made the cross of 16A threads.

Step 7: Pick up a shed with the left 4C and 8A threads and weave the 4 upper left B threads through this shed to left center.

Step 8: Pick up a shed with these left 4B threads, the right 8A and 4C threads and weave the 4 upper right B threads through this shed to left center. This makes the second cross of 8B threads.

Step 9: Now there is a group of 4C threads on the upper left and the upper right sides. Weave each C group through the respective sheds to cross in the middle. This cross of the C color makes a dot in the middle of the diamond of colors A and B.

Step 10: Before you can cross the B groups to complete the B diamond, you must weave each group of 4C threads through sheds made up of 4 color B and 8 color A threads first to the left and then to the right selvage.

Step 11: Now you can cross the B groups and weave them through the 8A groups on each side and on through the upper 4C groups (see Illus. 46).

Step 12: Cross the two right groups of 4A threads each through respective sheds of the left 8A threads, as you did above, and you have completed the lozenge. Continue this pattern to your desired length.

Study the design to learn to judge what step you are required to make to bring the succeeding color crosses to the center. You will also discover that you can create other designs using the crossing technique.

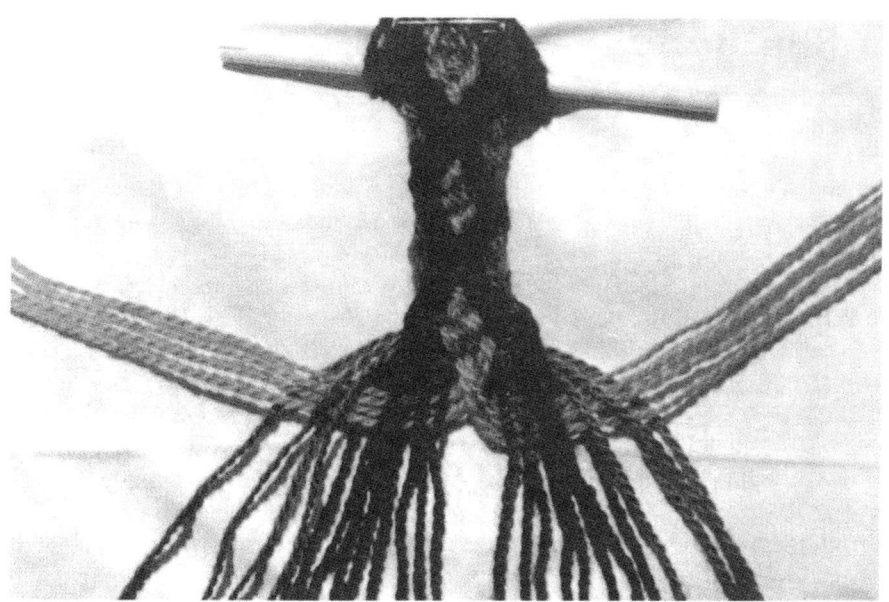

Illus. 46. This step in weaving the three-color Peruvian cross rep with multiple wefts and single warps shows the crossing of the lower small diamond (B) threads. Next, cross the A threads in the center to complete the large lozenge.

Peruvian Rep Braid

(Multiple Wefts, Single Warps;
Single Wefts, Multiple Warps)

In the Peruvian method of using multiple threads of weft as one weft alone, you have considerable freedom for exposing or covering certain color areas. When you are familiar with the preceding three Peruvian designs, let your imagination carry you on to other possibilities. For simple experimental purposes, try the following pattern.

Arrange threads 2⅓ yards long on a dowel in the order: 4 light A, 4 light B, 4 light A, 4 dark C, 4 dark D, 4 dark C.

Step 1: Start from the left and weave the group of 4 light A threads over and under single warp threads towards the right edge. Weave the next left group of light threads (B group) to the right using a shed of single warp threads and include the 4A threads already woven as a multiple weft as single warps.

Weave the group of left 4 light A threads to the right through a shed of single warps including the 4B threads you just placed there. Now the dark threads are on the left and the light threads are on the right.

Step 2: Weave with the left group of 4 dark C threads under and over single warp threads to the right including the 4 dark D, 4 dark C and all of the light threads. Do the same with the second dark group, color D, always including in the warp on the right each succeeding group of threads which you have already used as a weft.

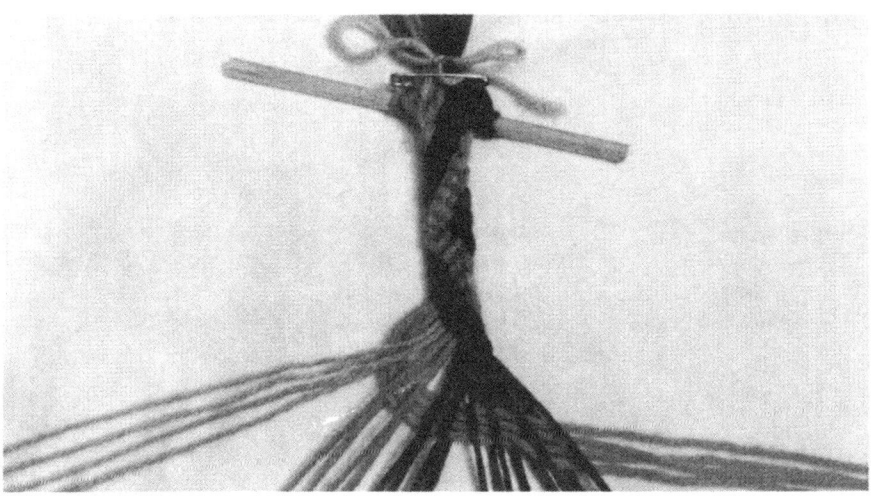

Illus. 47. This Peruvian rep braid shows one completed pattern and the beginning of the next. Experiment with color and direction for imaginative braids.

When you have woven each of the six groups of 4 threads each through to the right and have used them again as single warps, notice that you have started a diagonal design. You now have a choice relating to your design. You may continue the light diagonal design in the same way, or you may make a change of design by reversing the direction of the light stripe, turning it from upper right to lower left. To do this, you need to cover the dark threads with the light ones. You have observed that when you use single warps and multiple wefts, the weft threads are covered. The same is true if you use single wefts through groups of multiple warps—only the weft color shows and the multiple warps are covered.

Symmetry of Design

There is another factor to consider here besides having all of the light threads exposed from left to right. The design is more symmetrical if you let the 4B threads cover the left 4A threads by moving the B color to the left selvage before you start to move all of the single light threads through the multiple warps to the right.

Step 3: To cover the left outside 4A threads by color B, weave each single B thread over and under the group of 4A threads on the left. Now you have moved the B color to the left selvage. Placed there, it makes a symmetrical design which becomes more pronounced when you have woven the single light threads all the way to the right.

To do this, weave each single thread of the 4A group (previously covered by the B color) over and under each group of four warps to the right.

Next, weave to the right each single thread of the 4B color through a shed of succeeding groups of four warps each, including the 4A group you just placed at the right.

Step 4: Do the same with single threads of the remaining group 4A on the left, weaving through a shed of groups of 4 warps used as one, carrying the thread to the right, including, at the right edge, the group of 4B threads. When you weave with single threads, the selvage is more regular if you observe which threads should cross over the first warp group and which ones should cross under.

Keep the tension rather loose when weaving with the single wefts as this part of the work tends to be tighter than areas woven with single warps and multiple wefts.

Step 5: Now you may make an opposing dark design the same as the light one you have just made. To do so, weave next with the 12 single dark threads of 4C 4D 4C, weaving each one in turn to the right through a shed of groups of 4 warps. The dark band moves to the left.

You must adjust the line of the D color by weaving the 4D threads singly over and under the 4C group on the right (just as you did in Step 3) in order to make a symmetrical design.

Your threads are now in the same position as they were when you started.

Step 6: Repeat the design by starting now to weave with the left group of 4A threads—through a shed of single warps to the right (see Illus. 47). The dark band now begins to move from the right to the left again.

Weave each half of the belt to the desired length. Observe the design carefully as you proceed, in order to decide which color you want covered and which you want uncovered.

Peruvian Cross Rep Braid

(Multiple Wefts with Single Warps;
Single Wefts with Multiple Warps)

Arrange on a dowel 48 threads 2½ yards long in the following order: 4 light A, 4 light B, 4 light A, 4 dark C, 4 dark D, 8 dark C, 4 dark D, 4 dark C, 4 light A, 4 light B, 4 light A.

Step 1: With the left group of 4 light A threads, weave under and over single warps to the center. In the same way, weave the right group of 4 light A threads towards the left, under and over single warps, including the 4A threads you just wove from the left to the center. This procedure crosses the right and left groups of A threads in the center.

Step 2: Weave with each of the six groups of multiple wefts to the center, first from the left and then from the right. Each matching group of weft threads from the left and right always crosses in the center.

Symmetrical Choice

Just as you did in Step 3 of the preceding chapter, you need to adjust the line of the B color if you wish to make a symmetrical design.

Step 3: To reverse the light design or turn it in an opposite direction, you must now weave with single wefts through sheds made up of groups of warps of 4 threads each. Use each thread of the light colors singly through the multiple warp groups *from each side* crossing the left group with the *single* right warps at the center. Then use the same process with each of the 12 single dark threads on the left and on the right, weaving each thread through a shed made up of warp groups of 4 threads each. Cross the matching groups in the center.

Now the threads are in the same position as in the beginning (see Illus. 48).

Step 4: Repeat the process of first weaving with multiple wefts (4 in each group) through a shed of single warps from the left to the center and from the right to the center. Always cross matching groups in the center. Then weave single wefts through sheds made up of multiple warps (4 in each group) from left to right and from right to left. Always cross in the center.

Step 5: Weave each half of belt to the desired length. If you practice this useful technique further, you will learn to weave, with your own choice of colors, many varied geometric designs.

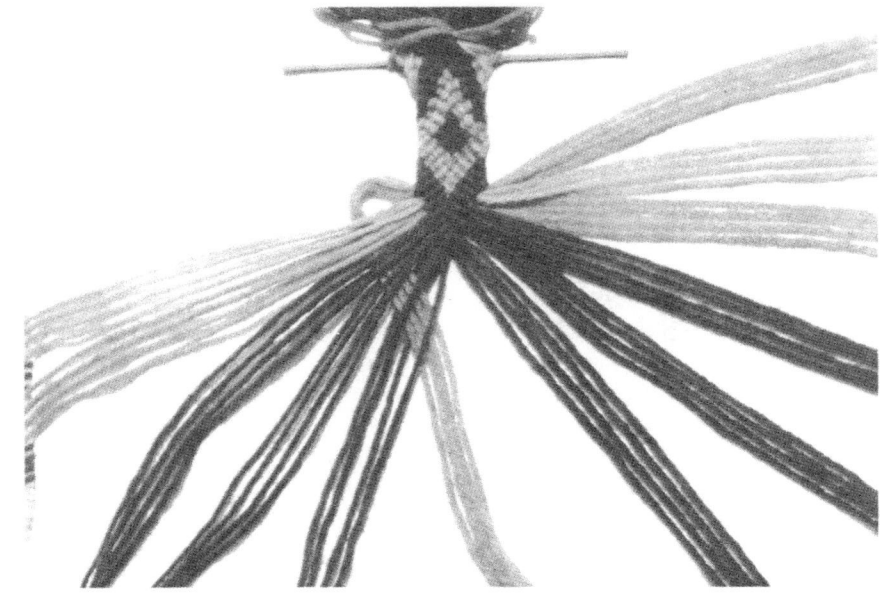

Illus. 48. This is a Peruvian cross rep braid woven with multiple wefts and single warps and then with multiple warps and single wefts. One pattern has been completed and the second is just beginning.

After You Finish

Now that you have learned the finger-weaving technique, be imaginative. Vary the length, width, colorations, and designs from those presented here and you will undoubtedly discover innumerable striking combinations you can weave with your fingers.

For additional inspiration and historical interest, you could visit museums that have finger woven flat braids to see authentic ancient prehistoric pieces. This might give you unusual ideas for color and design variations.

When you become an experienced finger weaver, perhaps you would enjoy teaching the craft—to friends or relatives, to children, to hospital patients, or to anyone who happens to be sitting next to you on a bus, train or plane. One day, you might even have the opportunity to teach an Indian boy or girl—from whose own ancestors this craft developed—how to finger weave a belt or neck-tie.

BIBLIOGRAPHY

The author would like to acknowledge the use of the following materials in the research for this book: *Byways in Handweaving* by Mary Meigs Atwater, The Macmillan Company, 1968; *The Primary Structures of Fabrics: An Illustrated Classification* by Irene Emery, The Textile Book Service, 1966; *Navaho Weaving, Its Technique & History* by Charles Avery Amsden, Rio Grande Press, 1964. The following additional materials were also used: *Handweaver & Craftsman,* Summer Issue, 1970, Assumption Sash by Adrienne Whitelaw; *Ojibwa Crafts* by Carrie A. Lyford, Bureau of Indian Affairs, 1943; *Paracas Fabrics and Nazca Needlework, 3rd Century* B.C. *to 3rd Century* A.D. by Junius Bird and Louisa Bellinger, The Textile Museum, Washington, D.C., 1954; *Textiles of Ancient Peru and Their Structures* by Raoul D'Harcourt, University of Washington Press, 1962; *The Cultivation and Weaving of Cotton in the Prehistoric Southwestern United States* by Kate Peck Kent, The American Philosophical Society, Philadelphia, 1957; *The Development of Braiding as a Decorative Art* (English translation) by S. Domyo, 1965; and two Swedish texts: *Dakkan Crafts of Lapland,* Almqvist & Wiksells, Sweden, 1971, and *Sydsamisk Slöjd (Lapp Home Crafts),* Västerbottens Museum, Umea, Sweden, 1969.

Your Project Notes:

Index

after you finish 46
arrow-head design 17, 34–35
Assumption sash 4

Basket Maker sashes 5

chevron designs 12, 18–19, 22, 23, 25
   neck-ties 13, 26–27
collar 15
Creek Indian sash 5

diagonal and reverse 8
diagonal stripe pattern
   for belt 7, 8, 10–11, 14
   for collar 15
diamond design 9, 28–29
   Creek Indian sash 5
double chevron design 13, 23
double diamond design 9
   Osage sash 8
double lightning design 16, 32–33

fringe, making of 14

interlocking technique 30

lightning design 16, 30–31

methods and materials 6

neck-ties 13, 26–27

North American Indian designs 7–19, 22–23, 25–35

Osage sash 8

Peruvian cross rep braid 21, 24
   multiple wefts with single warps;
     single wefts with multiple warps 44–45
   three colors, multiple wefts, single warps 40–41
   two colors, multiple wefts, single warps 38–39
Peruvian designs 20–21, 24, 36–45
Peruvian rep braid 20, 24
   multiple wefts, single warps 36–37
   multiple wefts, single warps; single wefts, multiple warps 42–43

shed 6

triple arrow-head design 17